BLACK TECH

LEADERS IN TECHNOLOGY

YESTERDAY, TODAY, AND TOMORROW

Theresa Merritt-Watson

BLACK TECH
Leaders in Technology
Yesterday, Today, And Tomorrow

Copyright ©2024 Theresa Merritt-Watson

Second Edition

All rights reserved. No part of this book may be reproduced or transmitted in any form or by any means electronic or mechanical. Including photocopying, recording or by any information storage and retrieval system, without written permission from the author.

Published by HOV Publishing,
a division of HOV, LLC.
Bridgeport, CT

Illustrator: Gerard A Harmon
Mass Social Media Group

For More Information, Contact:
Synergy Network LLC.
109 N. Graham Street, Suite 106
Chapel Hill, NC 27516
Tel: 919-274-2370
SynergyNetworkLLC1@gmail.com
SynergyNetworkLLC.com

ISBN: 978-1-955107-18-1 (paperback)
ISBN: 978-1-955107-17-4 (hard case)
ISBN: 978-1-955107-16-7 (digital)

Printed in the United States of America

This book is dedicated to my future self and my readers. Just know you are what you speak and what you tell yourself, so speak positive, fun, excitement, and truths and always lift yourself no matter what is going on.

To my children, parents, family, and friends, thank you for your affirmations; you help shape who I am.

BLACK TECH

LEADERS IN TECHNOLOGY

YESTERDAY, TODAY, AND TOMORROW

Acknowledgments

Special thanks to these educators and my friends:
    Ms. Gwen Atwater
    Dr. Saria Canady
    Dr. Joyce Roland
    Dr. Janelle Weddington

BLACK TECH

LEADERS IN TECHNOLOGY

YESTERDAY, TODAY, AND TOMORROW

Theresa Merritt-Watson

Equity and Equality for All

BLACK TECH

LEADERS IN TECHNOLOGY

YESTERDAY, TODAY, AND TOMORROW

Eagle

We used the eagle on the cover because it symbolizes loyalty, devotion, freedom, truth, honor, the divine, hope, foresight, and spiritual awareness.

The eagle's characteristics are the same traits we need for critical thinking, problem-solving, and creativity. The inventors featured in this book possessed these traits, transferring their knowledge and experiences to create inventions we still use today. Some of these inventors are still with us, continuing to inspire future generations.

My grandparents live far away, but Jesse Russell's invention lets me talk to them from anywhere in world.

10

Jesse Eugene Russell

Invention: The modern cell phone.
Born in Nashville, Tennessee, on April 26, 1948.
Attended: Tennessee State University,
 Nashville, Tennessee-HBCU.

My parents and I travel to lots of new places. We never get lost, thanks to Gladys West's invention.

Gladys West

Invention: Global Positioning System (GPS).
Born in Sutherland, Virginia, on October 27, 1930.
Attended: Virginia State University,
    Petersburg, Virginia-HBCU.

When I grow up, I want to be an astronaut. I will take pictures of the moon from space with George Carruthers's invention.

George Robert Carruthers

Invention: Ultraviolet Camera or spectrograph for Apollo 16.

Born in Cincinnati, Ohio, on October 1, 1939, and lived until December 26, 2020.

Attended: University of illinois Urbana-Champaign, Champaign, Illinois.

When I visit my aunt in Chicago during the winter holidays, it's windy and cold outside. However, my aunt's house is always warm and cozy because of Alice Parker's invention.

Alice Parker

Invention: Patented a natural gas furnace in 1919. Her invention helped modernize the HVAC industry and central heating systems.
Born in Morristown, New Jersey, in 1895 and lived until 1920.
Attended: Howard University, Washington, District of Columbia-HBCU.

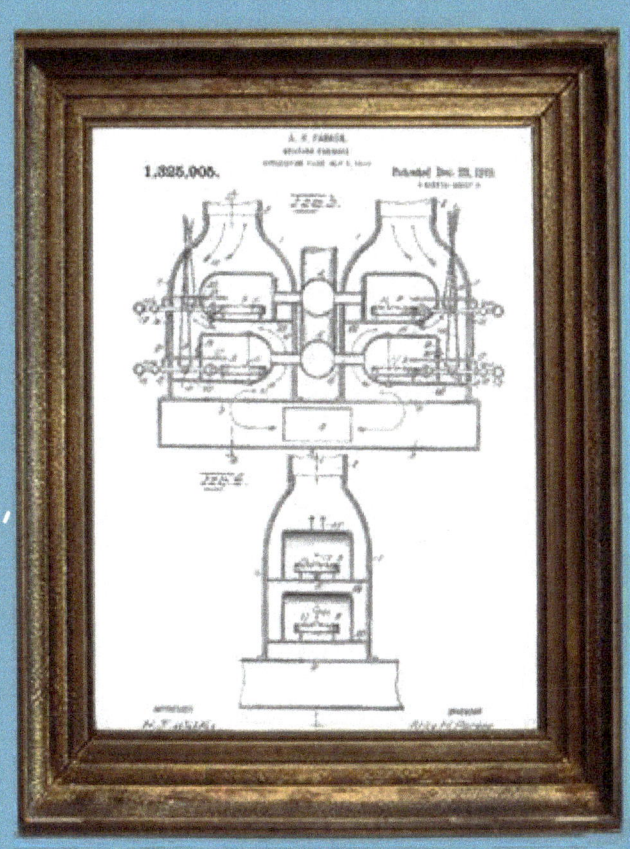

I love movies, especially when the characters jump out at me. I can use Kenneth J. Dunkley's invention to see the special effects.

Kenneth J. Dunkley

Invention: 3D glasses.
Born in New York, New York,
 on December 29. 1939.
Attended: New York University,
 New York.

My favorite television and movie characters seem life like with Valerie Thomas's invention.

Valerie Thomas

Invention: 3D illusion transmitter.
Born in Baltimore, Maryland, on February 8, 1943.
Attended: Morgan State University, Baltimore, Maryland-HBCU.

When I go work with my dad, I get excited to ride all the way to the 10th floor. I press all the buttons just to see the elevator doors open. We no longer need a person to open the elevator doors for us. Thanks to Alexander Miles's invention, we get to my dad's office easily.

Alexander Miles

Invention: Automatic elevator door opener and closer. His invention required no help from the operator or passenger.

Born in Pickaway County, Ohio, on May 18, 1838, and lived until May 7, 1918.

Education: He was a self-taught engineer.

I still use paper and pencil to solve math problems because Mary W. Jackson impressed me with her mathematical skills as a human computer.

Mary W. Jackson

Invention: She was a mathematician and aerospace engineer. She was the first black female engineer at NASA.

Born in Hampton, Virginia, on April 9, 1921, and lived until February 11, 2005.

Attended: Hampton University, Hampton, Virginia-HBCU.

Ice cream is my favorite dessert from the local grocery store. It gets delivered to the store without melting because of Frederick Jones's invention.

Frederick Jones

Invention: Refrigeration truck used to transport blood, food, and medicine during World War II.

Born in Cincinnati, Ohio, on May 17, 1893, and lived until February 21, 1961.

Education: Self-taught mechanical and electrical engineer.

When I had to go to virtual school, I could see and talk to my teachers online because of Marian R. Croak's invention.

Marian R. Croak

Invention: Voice over Internet Protocol (VoIP), which enables us to make calls over the internet instead of a phone line.
Born in New York, New York, on May 14, 1955.
Attended: Princeton University, Princeton, New Jersey.

Sometimes, I'm afraid of the dark, but I can keep a little light on in my room all night, thanks to Lewis Latimer's invention.

Lewis Howard Latimer

Invention: Light bulb filament, which allows your lights to stay on longer.

Born in Chelsea, Massachusetts, on September 4, 1848, and lived until December 11, 1928.

Education: Self-taught engineer.

When someone comes to visit, we can see who is outside before letting them in. Marie Van Brittan-Brown's invention makes this possible.

Marie Van Brittan-Brown

Invention: Protype for closed-circuit television security known as your home security system.

Born in Jamaica, Queens, New York, on October 30, 1922, and lived until February 2, 1999.

Attended: Harrison College.

When traveling to my school, Garrett Morgan's invention helps us to get there safely. It tells us when to slow down, stop, and go.

Garrett Morgan

Invention: Traffic Light.
Born in Paris, Kentucky, on March 4, 1877, and lived until July 27, 1963.
Education: Self-taught engineer.

When my parents use their computer for job opportunities and claims tracking, they can thank Janet Bashen for her invention that lets them do things faster and easier.

Janet E. Bashen

Invention: Web-based software solution. The first Black woman to receive a patent for a web-based software solution.

Born in Mansfield, Ohio, on February 12, 1957.

Attended: University of Houston, Houston, Texas.

Notes

1	Bashen, Janet	Janet Emerson Bashen (1957-), (blackpast.org).
2	Carruthers, George	George Carruthers receives Innovation Award, Document, Gale Academic OneFile (temple.edu).
3	Croak, Marian R.	Marian R. Croak Invented Technology so You can make a call using the computer, ProQuest.
4	Dunkley, Kenneth J	US4810057A, Three-Dimensional Viewing Glasses, Google Patents.
5	Jackson, Mary W.	Mary W. Jackson, NASA's First Female African American Engineer, NASA.
6	Jones, Frederick	Frederick McKinley Jones, Inventor Born, African American Registry (aaregistry.org).
7	Latimer, Lewis	Lewis Latimer, Lemelson (mit.edu).
8	Miles, Alexander	Alexander Miles, Lemelson (mit.edu).
9	Morgan, Garrett	Garrett Morgan, Patents Three-Position Traffic Signal, History.
10	Parker, Alice	"What We Know about Alice Parker, a 'Hidden Figure' in Modern Heating," Energy News Network.
11	Russell, Jesse Eugene	Jesse Russell, cell phone inventor, Born African American Registry (aaregistry.org).
12	Thomas, Valerie	Valerie Thomas, Lemelson (mit.edu).
13	Van Brittan-Brown, Mary	Marie Van Brittan-Brown (mit,edu).
14	West, Gladys	Gladys West (scientificwomen.net).

BLACK TECH

LEADERS IN TECHNOLOGY

YESTERDAY, TODAY, AND TOMORROW

Interactive Section

Interactive Content

1. Match the Inventors
2. Unscramble the Words
3. Inventors Word Puzzle
4. Inventor Questions
5. Puzzle Word Search
6. Inventors Education
7. Create Your Invention
8. Inventors Coloring Book

Match the Inventor to the Invention

INVENTORS	INVENTIONS
1. Janet Bashen	GPS
2. Lewis Latimer	Security System
3. Mary Jackson	Automatic Elevator Door Opener
4. Marian Croak	Modern Cell Phone
5. Gladys West	Refrigeration Truck
6. Alice Parker	Light Bulb Filament
7. Mary Van-Brittan Brown	Traffic Light
8. Federick Jones	Voice Over Internet Protocol (VOIP)
9. Jesse Russell	Gas Furnace
10. Garrett Morgan	3-D Illusion Transmitter
11. Alexander Miles	Web-based Software
12. George Carruthers	3-D Glasses
13. Valerie Thomas	Ultraviolet Camera
14. Kenneth Dunkley	Mathematician

Unscramble Words

1. GLEAE _____

2. IRRREAGTOFER _____

3. HLTIG _____

4. RIFTFAC _____

5. BBUL _____

6. LNAETFMI _____

7. BWE _____

8. SOILIULN _____

ANSWER KEY:
1. EAGLE
2. REFRIGERATOR
3. LIGHT
4. TRAFFIC
5. BULB
6. FILAMENT
7. WEB
8. SOLUTION

Inventors Word Puzzle

R	U	S	S	E	L	L
A	P	Z	X	R	P	J
J	A	C	K	S	O	N
T	R	K	R	N	N	X
R	K	M	E	O	Q	A
L	E	W	I	S	A	K
W	R	M	A	R	Y	K

Jackson   Mary   Jones   Lewis

Parker   Croak   Russell

Inventor Questions

1. Who invented the Ultraviolet Camera for space
   _____

2. What does GPS stand for _____

3. What did Lewis Latimore Invent

   _____

4. Who created VOIP making zoom possible

   _____

5. Who delivered medicine _____

6. You don't need anyone to help with opening

   the _____ doors

7. Who invented the traffic light

   _____

Puzzle Word Search

F	I	L	A	M	E	N	T	I	X
J	H	V	C	H	Z	X	L	L	C
I	C	X	Y	W	H	L	I	L	E
V	N	N	Z	G	E	F	G	A	L
B	D	T	T	K	Q	S	H	T	L
A	E	H	E	Z	Z	Q	T	I	P
S	E	C	U	R	I	T	Y	M	H
H	F	V	E	R	N	I	G	E	O
E	I	I	M	I	L	E	S	R	N
N	P	M	H	U	V	K	T	E	E

Cellphone   Internet   Security

Light   Latimer   Filament

West   Bashen   Miles

Inventors Education

Historical Black Colleges and Universities (HBCU)

Hampton University	Mary Jackson
Tennessee State University	Jesse Eugene Russell
Virginia State University	Gladys West
Howard University	Alice Parker
Morgan State University	Valerie Thomas

Self-Taught Inventors

Elevator Door Opener	Alexandria Miles
Refrigerator Truck	Frederick Jones
Light Filament	Lewis Latimer
Traffic Light	Garrett Morgan

Create Your Invention

Write about your Passion, Interest, and Invention.

_____

_____

_____

_____

_____

_____

_____

_____

_____

Black Tech
Leaders In Technology
Yesterday, Today, and Tomorrow
Book Cover

Eagle

Jesse Eugene Russell

Invented the modern cell phone.

Jesse Eugene Russell invented the modern cell phone

Valerie Thomas Invented the 3D illusion transmitter

Frederick Jones Invented the Refrigeration Truck

Garrett Morgan invented the Traffic Light

About the Author

Theresa Merritt-Watson is committed to equity for all. She believes that equity and equality can begin with African American children knowing their history and the contributions that African Americans made to the development of this country. This knowledge can be unifying. Unity in the community is the way African Americans can continue to move forward and build on the foundation left by our ancestors. Every child has passion, wonder, and interests that must be nurtured at home, school, and church, and her book can help begin to foster the process.

African-American history should be part of a child's daily reading regimen. Knowing one's history benefits everyone and ensures that no one is left in the dark. It is of the utmost importance that children learn history from home. Theresa is advocating for black history to be a daily journey to include the good, bad, ugly, and indifferent. She believes that learning one's history can help children know themselves and that it can change the trajectory of African American education and economics. It will also invoke a sense of pride and patriotism.

BLACK TECH

LEADERS IN TECHNOLOGY

YESTERDAY, TODAY, AND TOMORROW

Books Coming Soon

1. Blacks in S.T.E.M
2. Blacks in MATHMATICS
3. Blacka in MUSIC
4. Black in POLITICS
5. Blacks in MEDICINE
6. Blacks in SCIENCE
7. Blacks in the ARTS
8. Blacks in ENGINEERING
9. Blacks in EDUCATION
10. Blacks in AVIATION
11. Blacks in FINANCE
12. Blacks in LITERATURE
13. Blacks in AGRICULTURE
14. Blacks in HOUSEHOLD ITEMS